THE COLORS IN FRENCH
Coloring While Learning French

Language Books for Grade 1
Children's Foreign Language Books

Speedy Publishing LLC
40 E. Main St. #1156
Newark, DE 19711
www.speedypublishing.com
Copyright 2017

All Rights reserved. No part of this book may be reproduced or used in any way or form or by any means whether electronic or mechanical, this means that you cannot record or photocopy any material ideas or tips that are provided in this book.

THE COLORS IN FRENCH
Coloring While Learning French

Language Books for Grade 1
Children's Foreign Language Books

Speedy Publishing LLC
40 E. Main St. #1156
Newark, DE 19711
www.speedypublishing.com
Copyright 2017

All Rights reserved. No part of this book may be reproduced or used in any way or form or by any means whether electronic or mechanical, this means that you cannot record or photocopy any material ideas or tips that are provided in this book.

Bonjour!
Let's learn colors in French!

Check out these color guides with the french translations.

Have fun with these coloring activities!

LES COLEURS

What color is this?

ENGLISH:

FRENCH

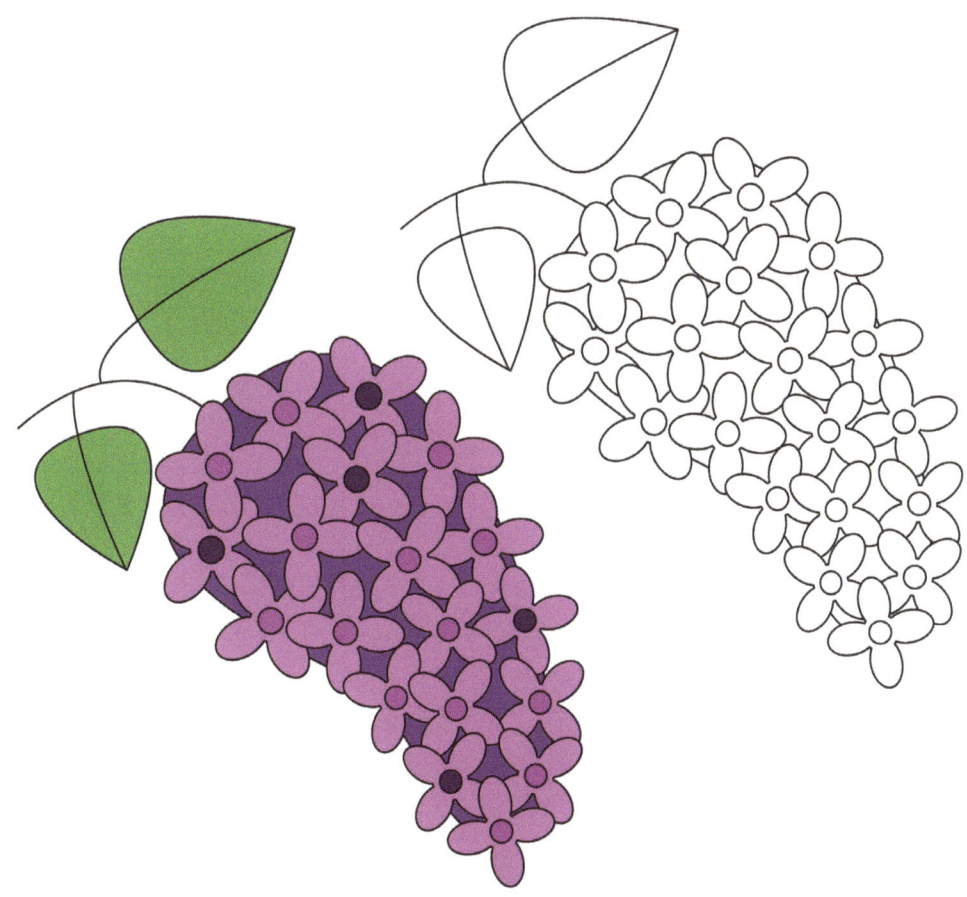

COLOR THE PICTURE!

ACTIVITY NO. 1

What color is this?

ENGLISH:

FRENCH:

COLOR THE PICTURE!

ACTIVITY NO. 2

What color is this?

ENGLISH:

FRENCH:

COLOR THE PICTURE!

ACTIVITY NO. 3

What color is this?

ENGLISH:

FRENCH:

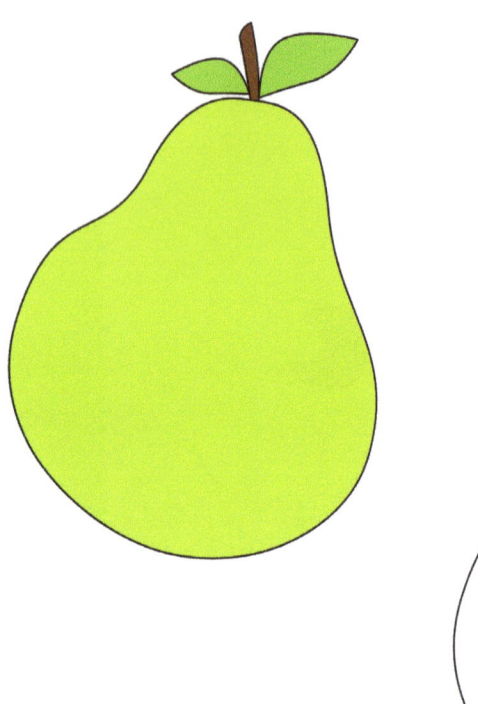
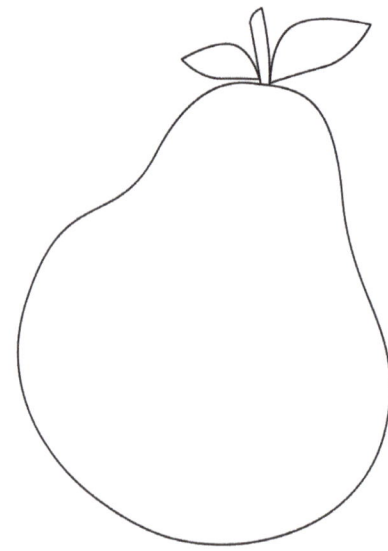

COLOR THE PICTURE!

ACTIVITY NO. 4

What color is this?

ENGLISH:

FRENCH

COLOR THE PICTURE!

ACTIVITY NO. 5

What color is this?

ENGLISH:

FRENCH:

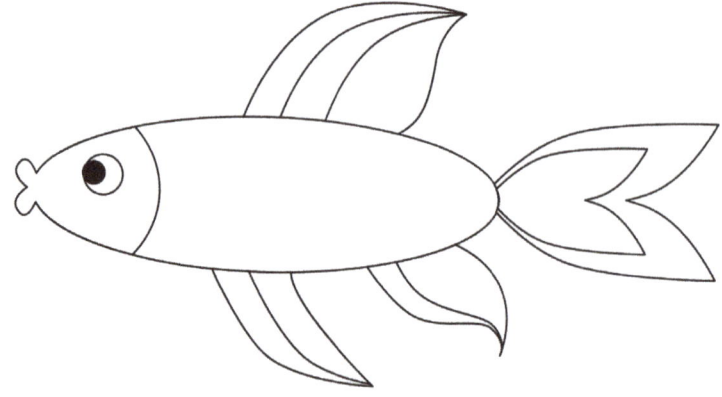

COLOR THE PICTURE!

ACTIVITY NO. 6

What color is this?

ENGLISH:

FRENCH:

COLOR THE PICTURE!

ACTIVITY NO. 7

What color is this?

ENGLISH:

FRENCH:

COLOR THE PICTURE!

ACTIVITY NO. 8

What color is this?

ENGLISH:

FRENCH

COLOR THE PICTURE!

ACTIVITY NO. 9

What color is this?

ENGLISH:

FRENCH:

COLOR THE PICTURE!

ACTIVITY NO. 10

What color is this?

ENGLISH:

FRENCH:

COLOR THE PICTURE!

ACTIVITY NO. 11

What color is this?

ENGLISH:

FRENCH:

COLOR THE PICTURE!

ACTIVITY NO. 12

What color is this?

ENGLISH:

FRENCH

COLOR THE PICTURE!

ACTIVITY NO. 13

What color is this?

ENGLISH:

FRENCH:

COLOR THE PICTURE!

ACTIVITY NO. 14

What color is this?

ENGLISH:

FRENCH

COLOR THE PICTURE!

ACTIVITY NO. 15

What color is this?

ENGLISH:

FRENCH:

COLOR THE PICTURE!

ACTIVITY NO. 16

What color is this?

| ENGLISH: | FRENCH |

COLOR THE PICTURE!

ACTIVITY NO. 17

What color is this?

ENGLISH:

FRENCH:

COLOR THE PICTURE!

ACTIVITY NO. 18

What color is this?

ENGLISH:

FRENCH:

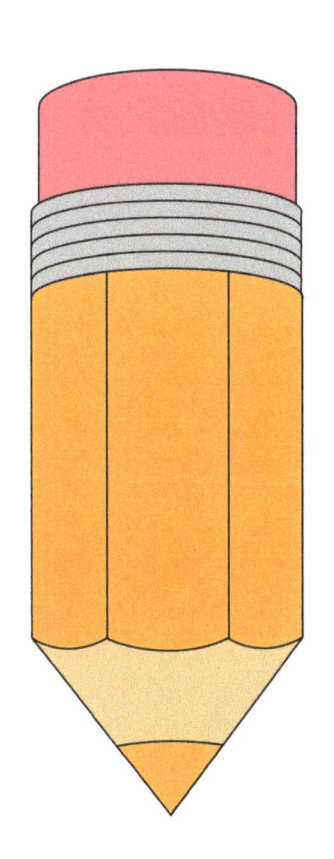

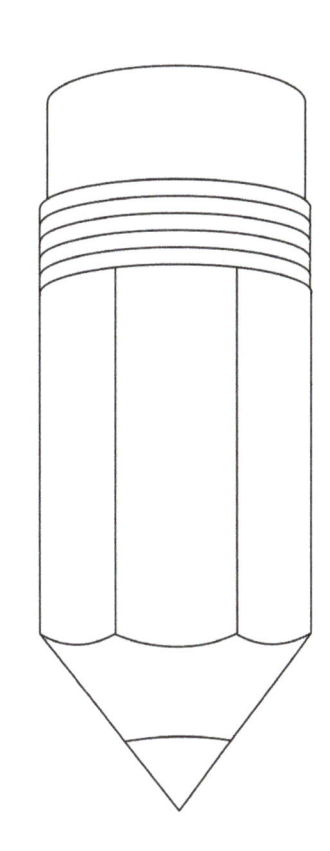

COLOR THE PICTURE!

ACTIVITY NO. 19

What color is this?

ENGLISH:

FRENCH:

COLOR THE PICTURE!

ACTIVITY NO. 20

What color is this?

| ENGLISH: | FRENCH |

COLOR THE PICTURE!

ACTIVITY NO. 21

What color is this?

ENGLISH:

FRENCH:

Sun

COLOR THE PICTURE!

ACTIVITY NO. 22

What color is this?

ENGLISH:

FRENCH:

COLOR THE PICTURE!

ACTIVITY NO. 23

What color is this?

ENGLISH:

FRENCH:

COLOR THE PICTURE!

ACTIVITY NO. 24

What color is this?

ENGLISH:

FRENCH

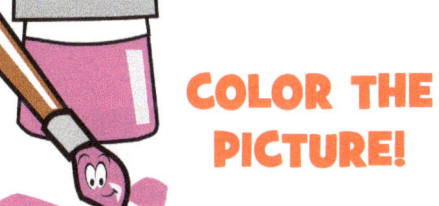

COLOR THE PICTURE!

ACTIVITY NO. 25

What color is this?

ENGLISH:

FRENCH:

COLOR THE PICTURE!

ACTIVITY NO. 26

What color is this?

ENGLISH:

FRENCH:

COLOR THE PICTURE!

ACTIVITY NO. 27

What color is this?

ENGLISH:

FRENCH:

COLOR THE PICTURE!

ACTIVITY NO. 28

What color is this?

ENGLISH:

FRENCH

COLOR THE PICTURE!

ACTIVITY NO. 29

What color is this?

ENGLISH:

FRENCH:

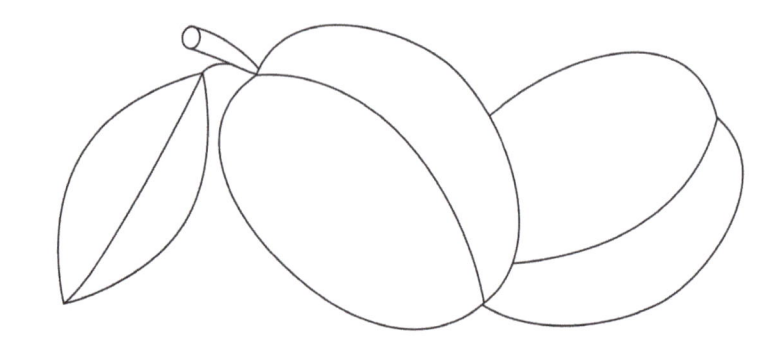

COLOR THE PICTURE!

ACTIVITY NO. 30

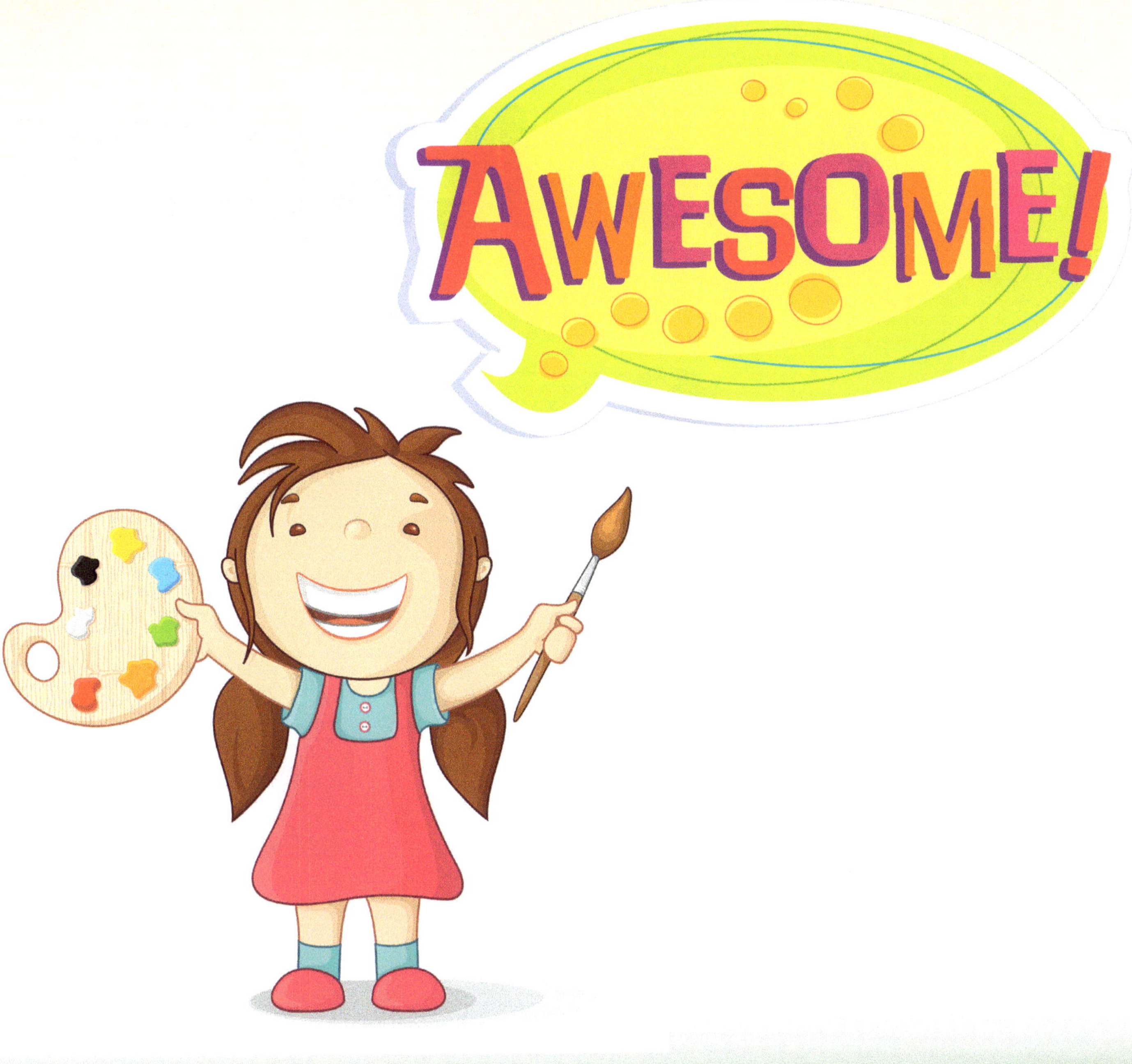
AWESOME!

ANSWERS

What color is this?

ENGLISH: Purple **FRENCH:** violet

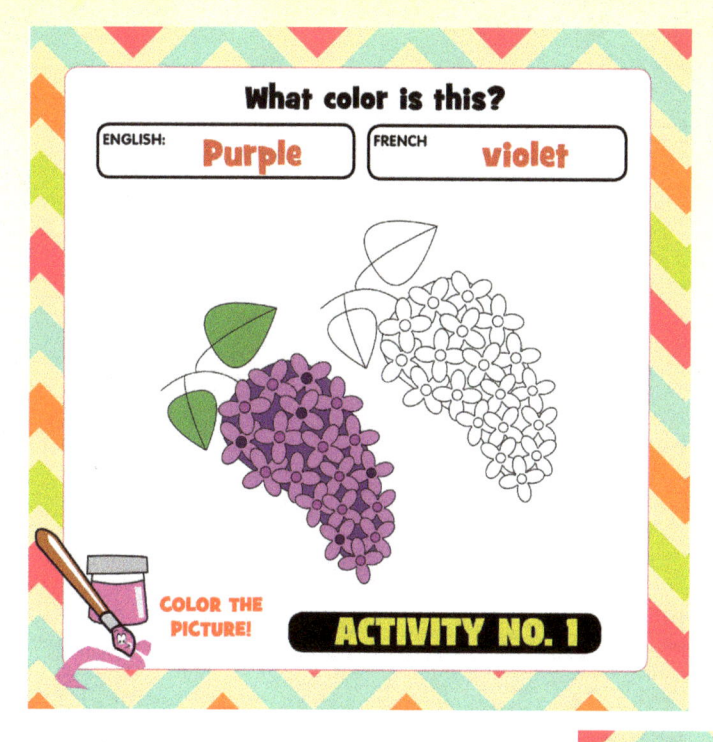

COLOR THE PICTURE!

ACTIVITY NO. 1

What color is this?

ENGLISH: Red **FRENCH:** Rouge

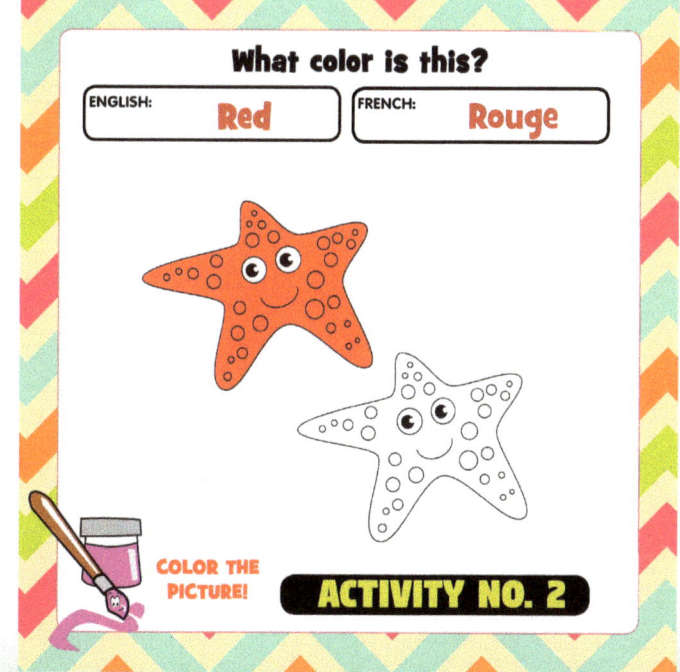

COLOR THE PICTURE!

ACTIVITY NO. 2

What color is this?

ENGLISH: Purple **FRENCH:** Violet

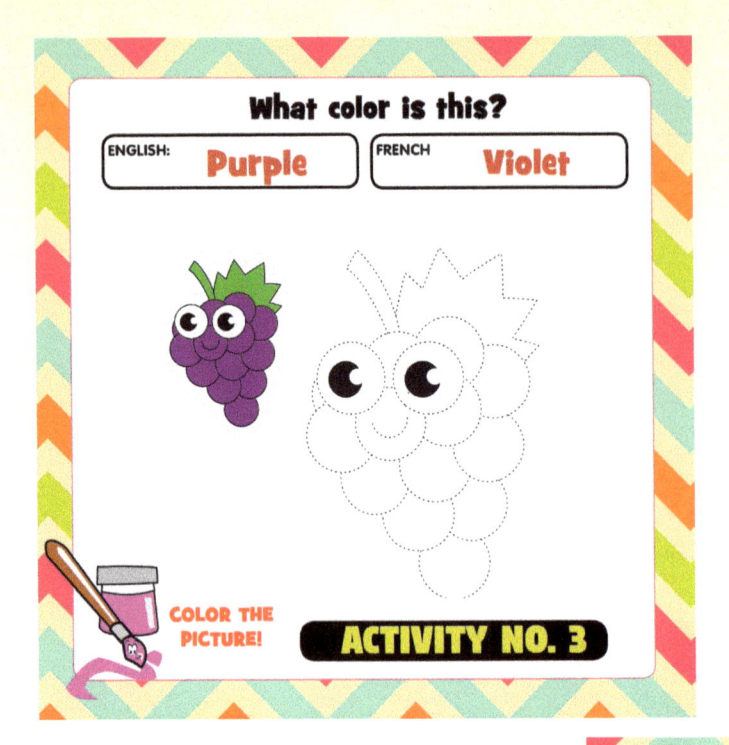

COLOR THE PICTURE!

ACTIVITY NO. 3

What color is this?

ENGLISH: Green **FRENCH:** Vert

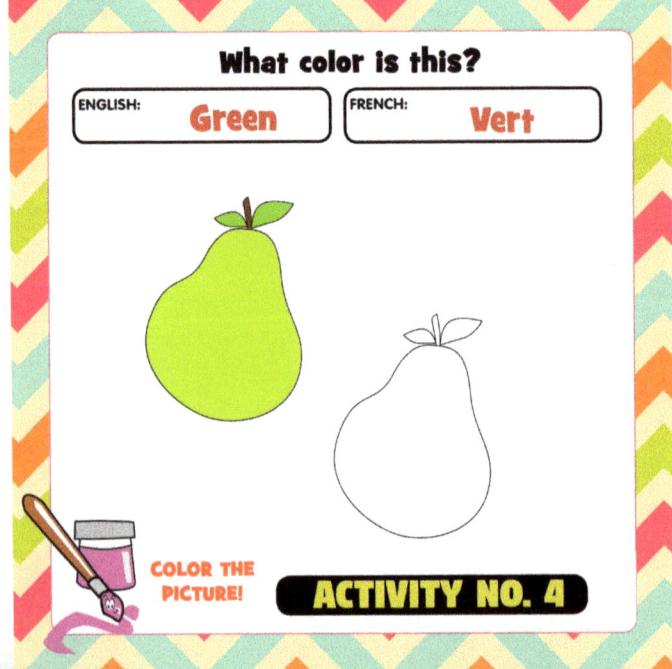

COLOR THE PICTURE!

ACTIVITY NO. 4

What color is this?

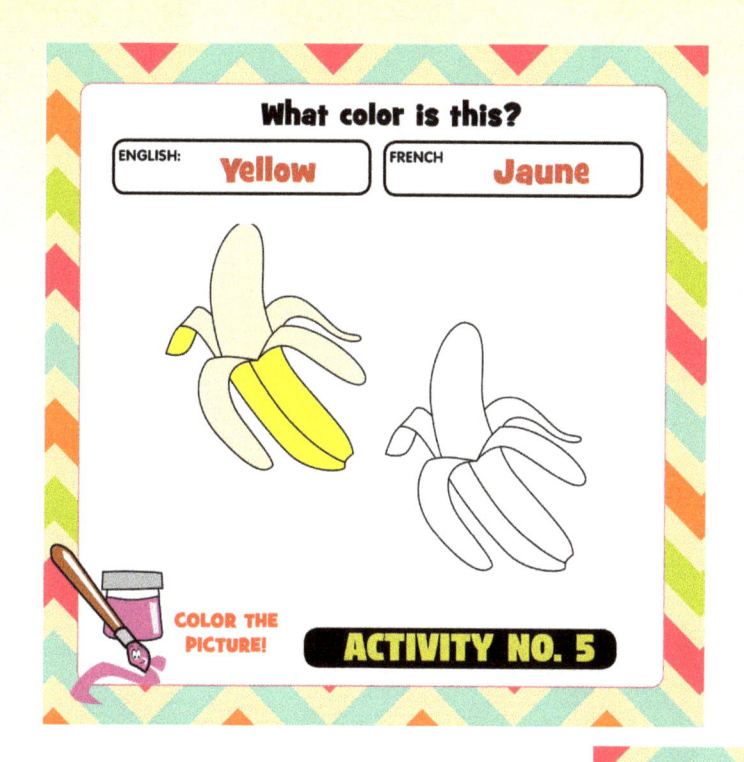

ENGLISH: Yellow **FRENCH:** Jaune

COLOR THE PICTURE!

ACTIVITY NO. 5

What color is this?

ENGLISH: Pink **FRENCH:** Rose

COLOR THE PICTURE!

ACTIVITY NO. 6

What color is this?

ENGLISH: Green **FRENCH:** Vert

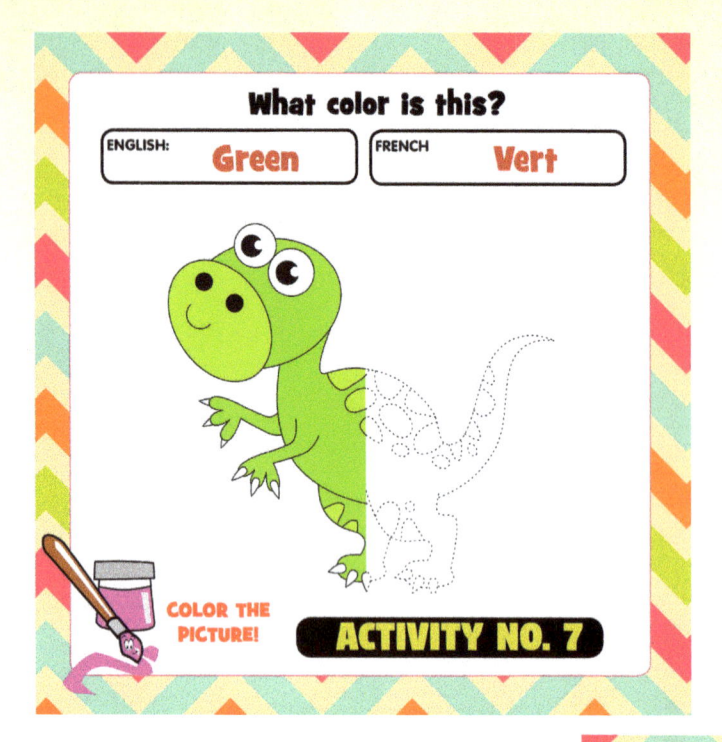

COLOR THE PICTURE!

ACTIVITY NO. 7

What color is this?

ENGLISH: Red **FRENCH:** Rouge

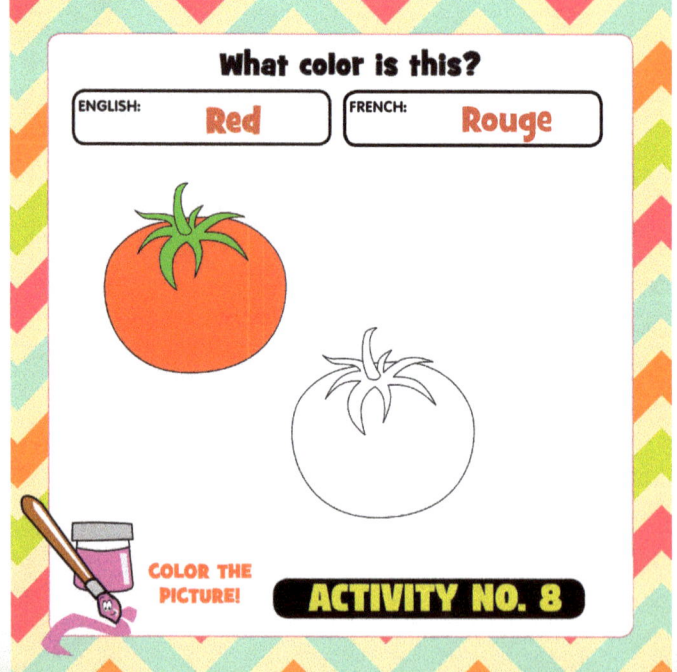

COLOR THE PICTURE!

ACTIVITY NO. 8

What color is this?

ENGLISH: Blue **FRENCH:** Bleu

Bese to be colored

COLOR THE PICTURE!

ACTIVITY NO. 9

What color is this?

ENGLISH: Orange **FRENCH:** Orange

COLOR THE PICTURE!

ACTIVITY NO. 10

What color is this?

ENGLISH: Yellow **FRENCH:** Jaune

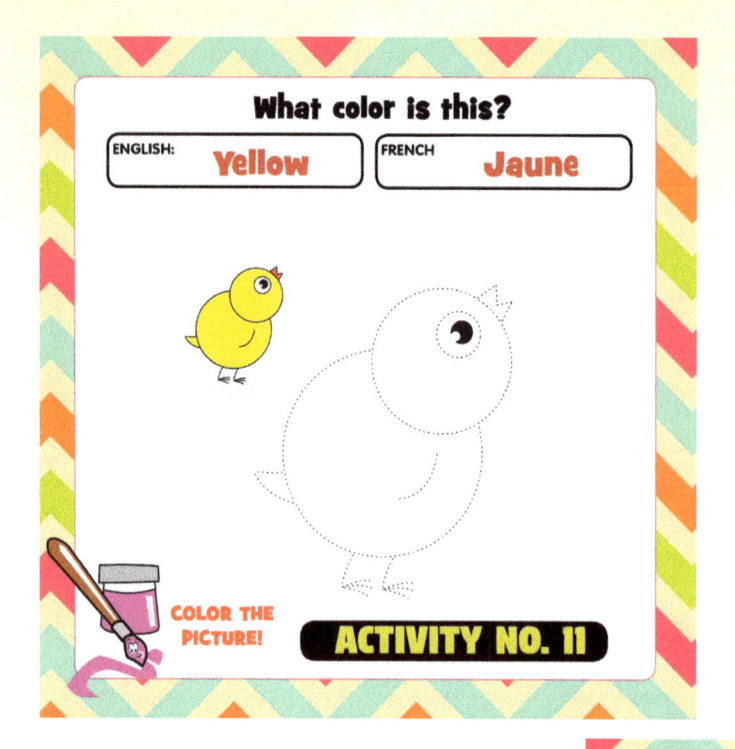

COLOR THE PICTURE!

ACTIVITY NO. 11

What color is this?

ENGLISH: Green **FRENCH:** Vert

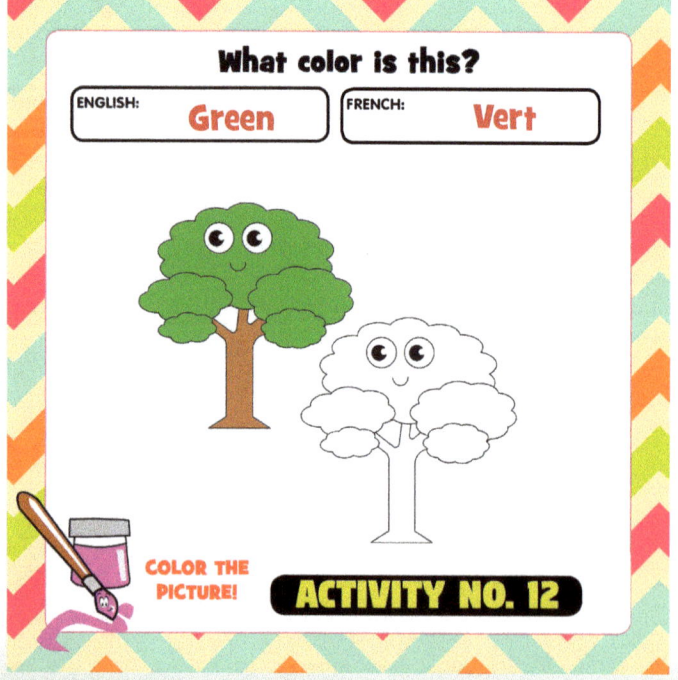

COLOR THE PICTURE!

ACTIVITY NO. 12

What color is this?

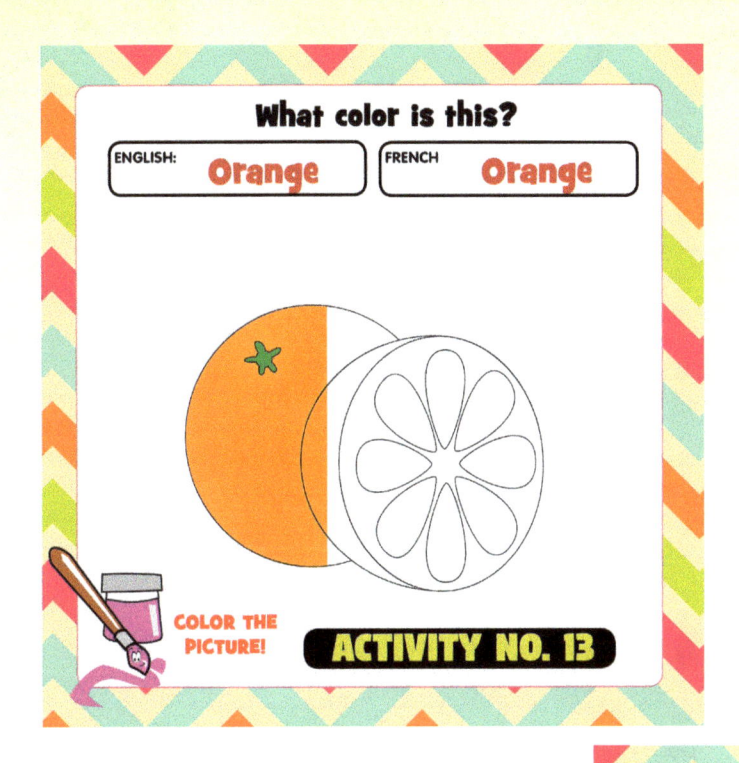

ENGLISH: Orange   **FRENCH:** Orange

COLOR THE PICTURE!

ACTIVITY NO. 13

What color is this?

ENGLISH: Yellow   **FRENCH:** Jaune

COLOR THE PICTURE!

ACTIVITY NO. 14

What color is this?

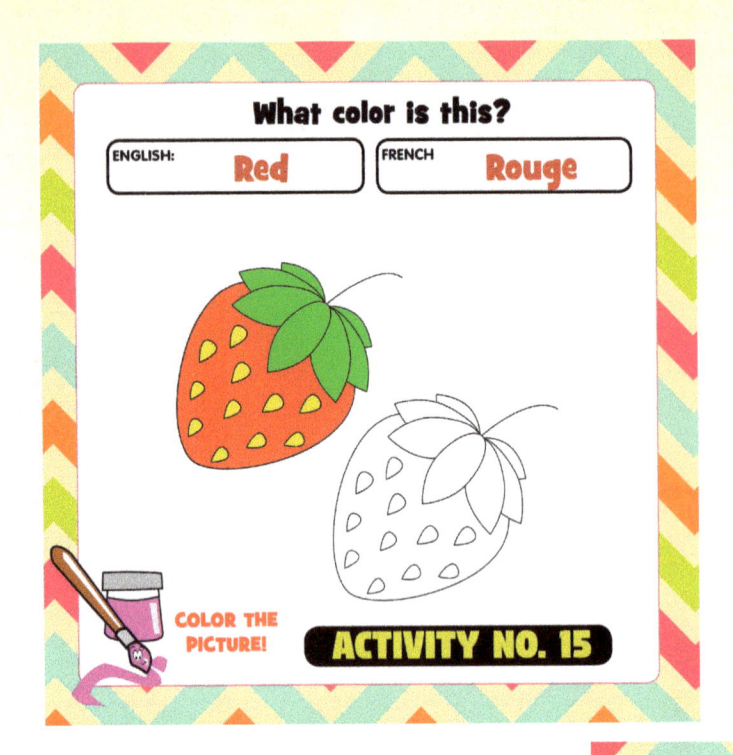

ENGLISH: Red **FRENCH:** Rouge

COLOR THE PICTURE!

ACTIVITY NO. 15

What color is this?

ENGLISH: Red **FRENCH:** Rouge

COLOR THE PICTURE!

ACTIVITY NO. 16

What color is this?

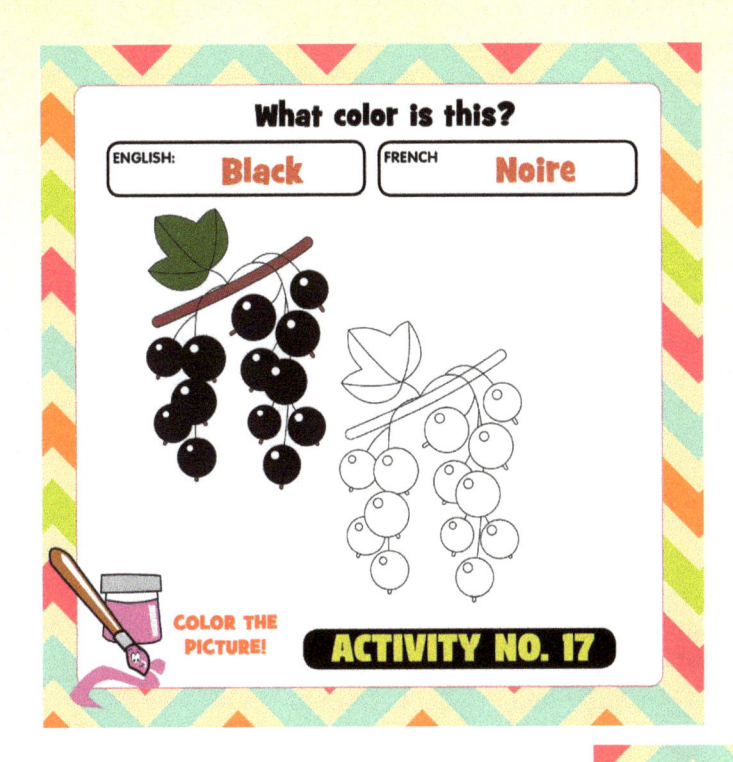

ENGLISH: Black **FRENCH:** Noire

COLOR THE PICTURE!

ACTIVITY NO. 17

What color is this?

ENGLISH: Brown **FRENCH:** Brun

COLOR THE PICTURE!

ACTIVITY NO. 18

What color is this?

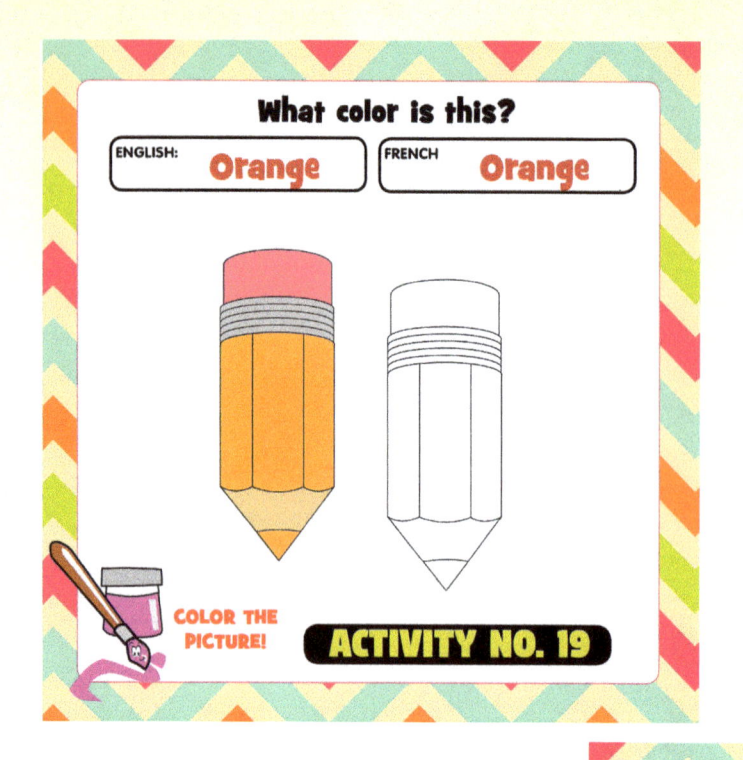

ENGLISH: Orange   **FRENCH:** Orange

COLOR THE PICTURE!

ACTIVITY NO. 19

What color is this?

ENGLISH: Blue   **FRENCH:** Bleu

COLOR THE PICTURE!

ACTIVITY NO. 20

What color is this?

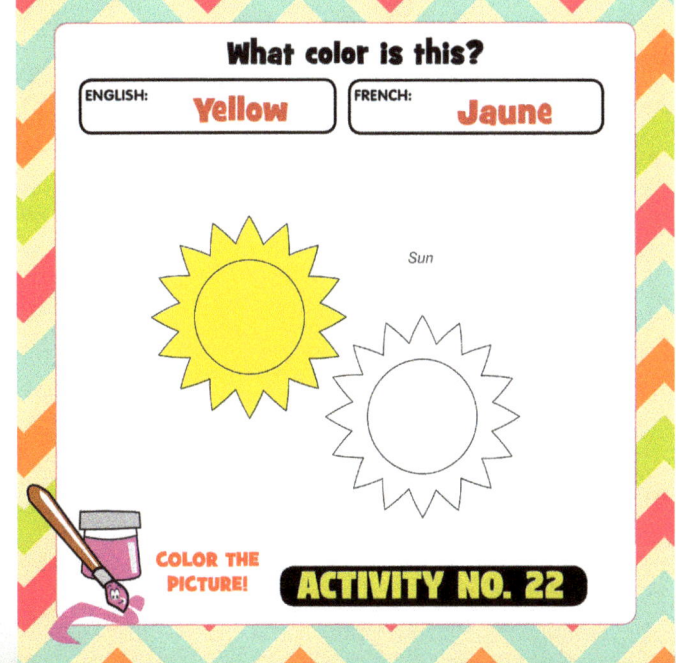

ENGLISH: Brown **FRENCH:** Brun

COLOR THE PICTURE!

ACTIVITY NO. 21

What color is this?

ENGLISH: Yellow **FRENCH:** Jaune

Sun

COLOR THE PICTURE!

ACTIVITY NO. 22

What color is this?

ENGLISH: Green **FRENCH:** Vert

COLOR THE PICTURE!

ACTIVITY NO. 23

What color is this?

ENGLISH: Green **FRENCH:** Vert

COLOR THE PICTURE!

ACTIVITY NO. 24

What color is this?

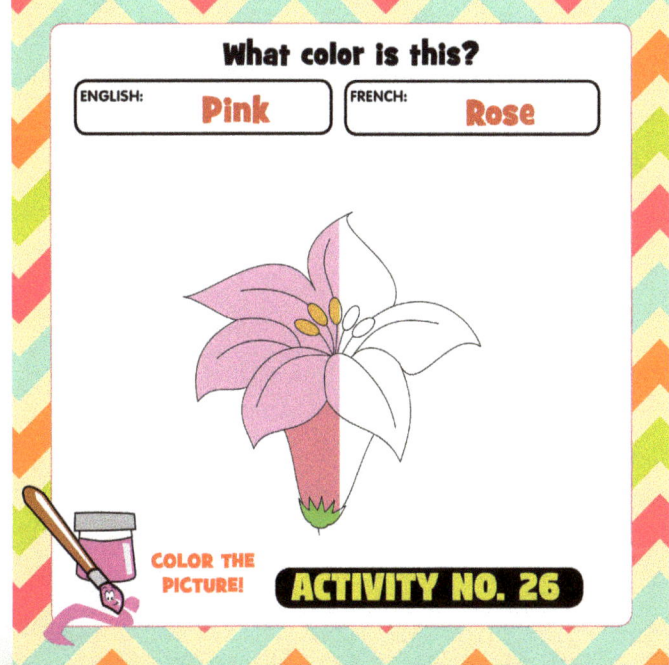

ENGLISH: Brown **FRENCH:** Brun

COLOR THE PICTURE!

ACTIVITY NO. 25

What color is this?

ENGLISH: Pink **FRENCH:** Rose

COLOR THE PICTURE!

ACTIVITY NO. 26

What color is this?

ENGLISH: Blue **FRENCH:** Bleu

COLOR THE PICTURE!

ACTIVITY NO. 27

What color is this?

ENGLISH: Purple **FRENCH:** Violet

COLOR THE PICTURE!

ACTIVITY NO. 28

What color is this?

ENGLISH: Orange **FRENCH:** Orange

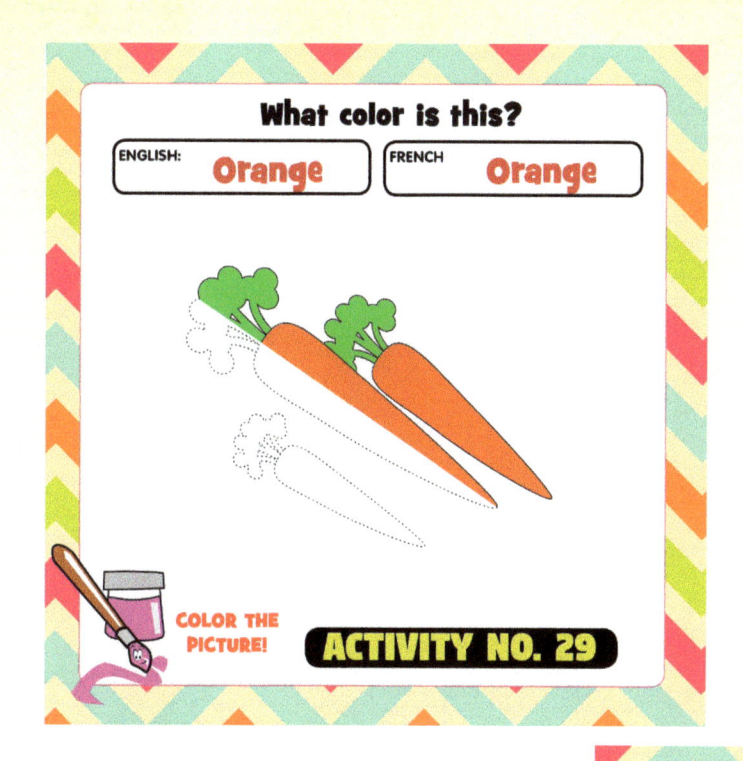

COLOR THE PICTURE!

ACTIVITY NO. 29

What color is this?

ENGLISH: Purple **FRENCH:** Violet

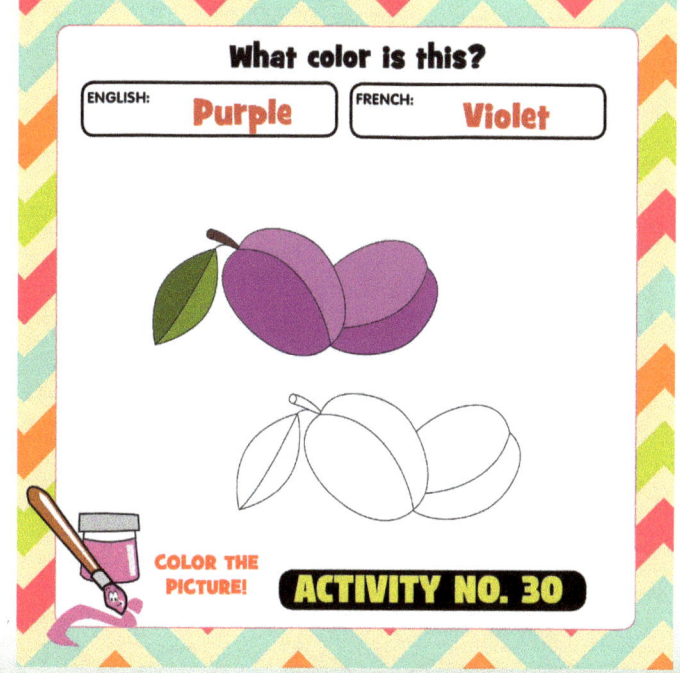

COLOR THE PICTURE!

ACTIVITY NO. 30

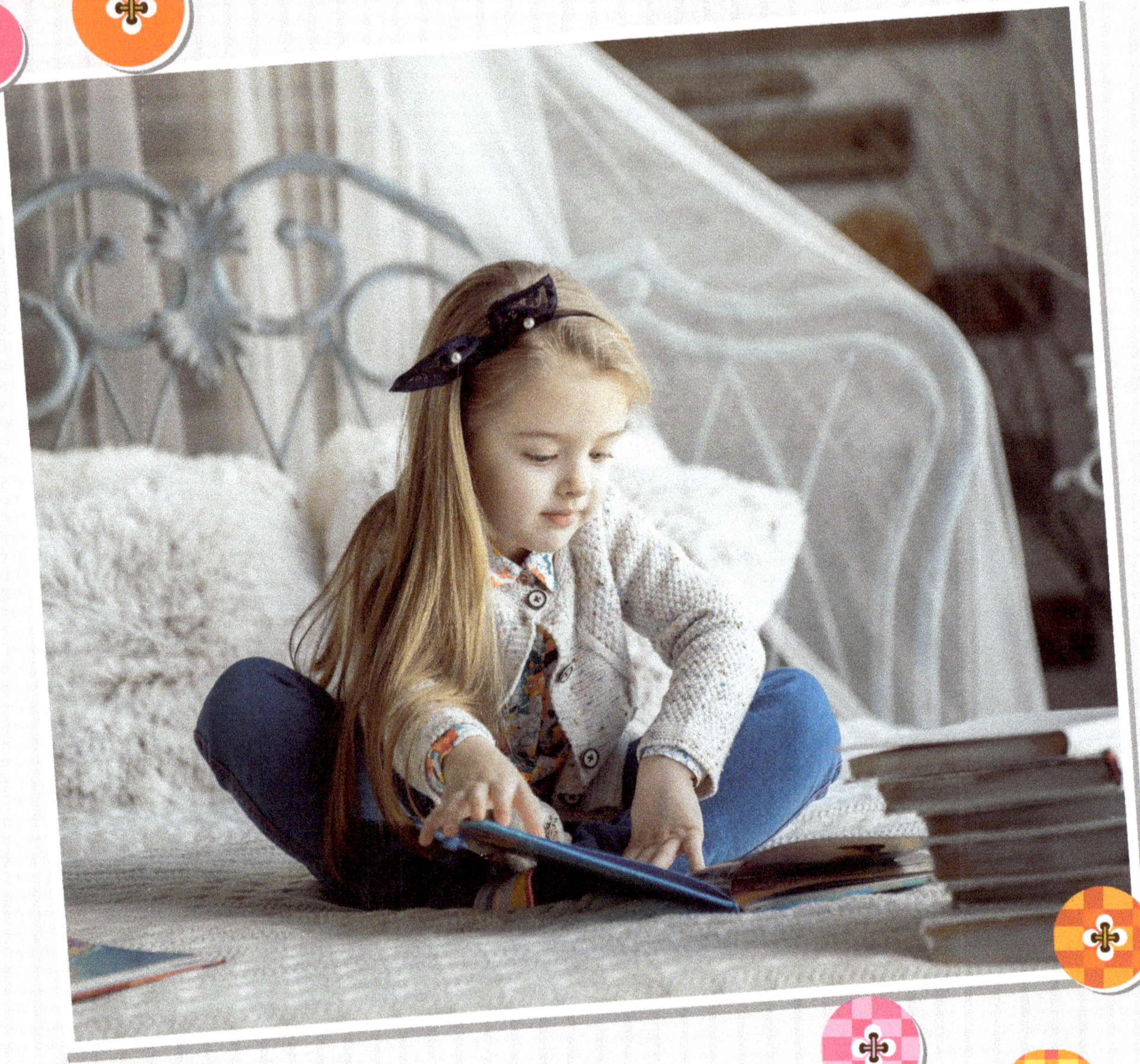

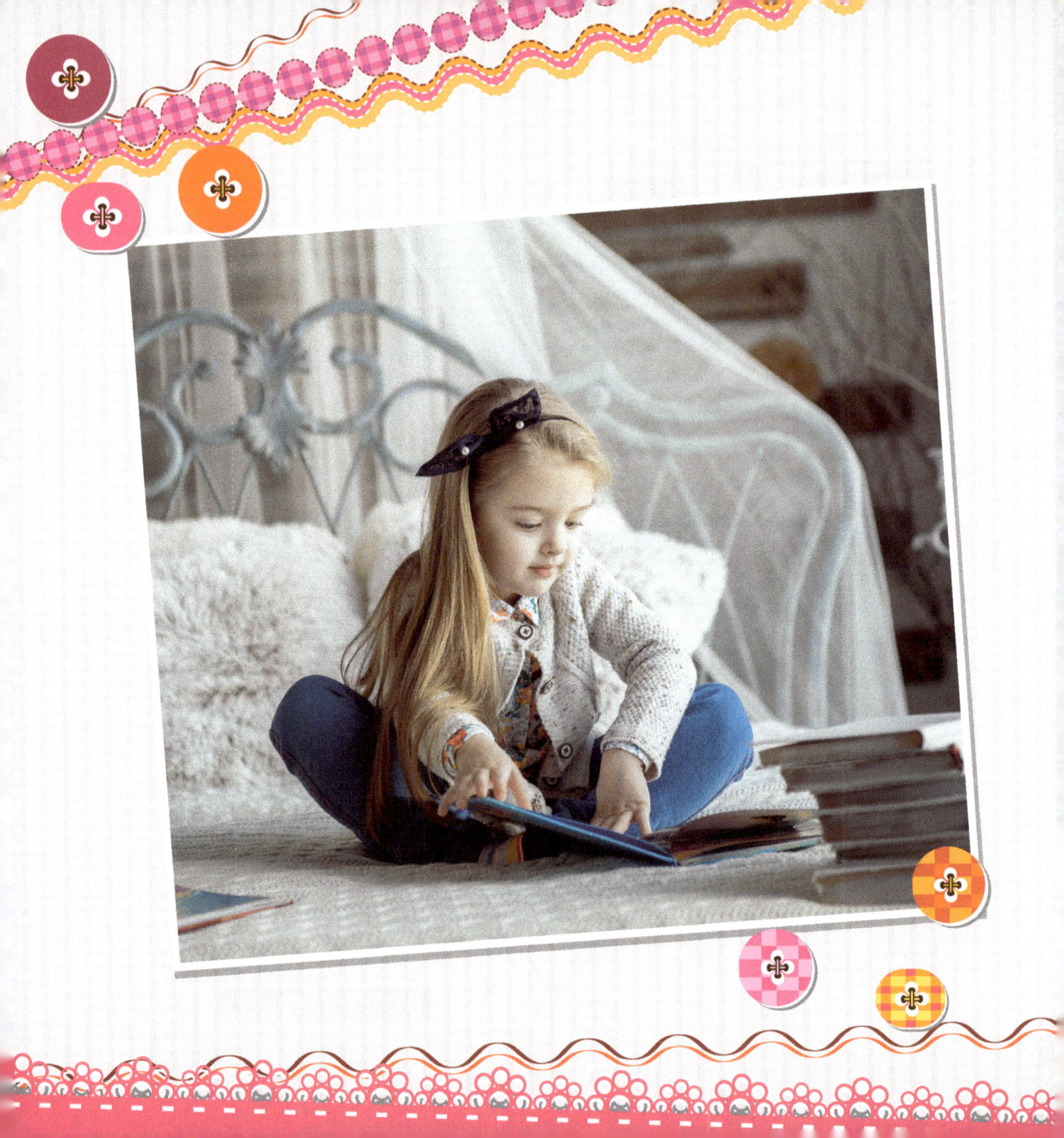

Visit

BABY PROFESSOR
EDUCATION KIDS

www.BabyProfessorBooks.com

to download Free Baby Professor eBooks
and view our catalog of new and exciting
Children's Books